SMILE

Bits and Pieces from my life to make you smile

By Eileen Henderson

Pen Press Publishers Ltd.

© **Eileen Henderson 2007**

All rights reserved

No part of this publication may be reproduced,
stored in a retrieval system, or transmitted
in any form or by any means, without
the prior permission in writing of the publisher,
nor be otherwise circulated in any form of binding or cover
other than that in which it is published and without a similar
condition including this condition being imposed on the
subsequent purchaser.

Published by Eileen Henderson

Pen Press Publishers Ltd
25 Eastern Place,
Brighton BN2 1NB

ISBN13: 978-1-905621-84-2

Printed and bound in the UK

Cover design by Jacqueline Abromeit

Dedication

My Thanks to my husband Frank, who patiently listened over the years, and to my family and friends. You all encouraged me enormously.

Without your escapades there could not have been a book.

Thank you all.

Yes - I did it!

Acknowledgments

My sincere thanks go to the following people who assisted in this production, their help means every penny goes to charity.

Mr. Goodheart who set the ball rolling, also some of my friends from Lombard, where some of the tales took place.

Andy Laing
John Clench
Alan Clarke
Joy and Kelvin Phillips
Julie Bass
Robin Westmoore
Ken Staff
The Zig Zag Golf Society

Fond memories.

Contents

INTRODUCTION

The Parky Club........	1
The Building Project........	4
Forty Years of Fun........	6
A Very Special Day........	10
My Jackdaws	12
A Tale of a Roaming Rascal........	15
Carnival Time down Tonbridge Way........	18
An Arresting Occasion.......	20
Hitching a Lift Down Under........	23
The Return.......	25
She is Off Again!........	26
Saturday Surprise........	27
Grandpa's 60th Birthday........	30
Welcome Home Marion!........	31
Lisa Comes of Age........	33
Some Come and Some Go........	36
For Karen — This is James's Life........	39
The Summer Of '54........	41
When Richard achieved his Half Century	45
It was James "The Irishman's" turn next	47
With this Ring........	49
Another Couple Tie The Knot........	50
Memories for Joy........	51
Waving Goodbye to Fiona........	54
The Wrinklies Lament........	56

A Christmas Tale........	57
The Garden........	62
The Big Birthday........	63
Caravanning - The Beginning........	67
Caravanning – part 2........	69
Caravanning - part 3........	71
Wardens at Play – (Slinfold Volunteers)...	73
Slinfold Volunteers 2........	76
What shall we do today dear?........	79
Halcyon Days........	81

Introduction

During my teenage years many conversations with my Father ended with us competing to compose suitable epitaphs for our gravestones. They were often irreverent, ghoulish or macabre and funny; we always ended up in fits of laughter. My Mother disapproved of our sense of humour, but I believe it is where my leanings towards rhyming words began.

After meeting my husband I learnt how to enjoy the pleasure of life which nature has given us. We walked many miles down country lanes, across fields and up and down hills, then teaching our two boys to do the same. From the boys escapades my stories began and was soon followed by poems.

Going to work in an office I was asked to write something for my colleagues to perform at our Christmas lunch. We had three Johns as managers, using them as targets I borrowed the tune White Christmas and wrote a saucy verse for each which two lovely young ladies dressed as Santas sang. They were so successful I was kept busy with requests for many events, birthdays, weddings, etc. Following my retirement from work I was diagnosed with Parkinson's Disease. I joined the local society where my talents came in useful at our New Year lunch.

While reading a poem called "The Parky Club" to our members, a friend looked in my folder and wondered why I hadn't shared these memories with others. He noted they are humorous and some saucy, designed to make you smile.

So, here they are! Smile Please!

This is a mixture of poems and tales of events from my life with family, friends and colleagues that made them laugh. Hopefully you will too!

I make no apology for starting with "The Parky Club". After printing costs are covered all proceeds will be donated to The Parkinson Society.

Eileen Henderson

The Parky Club

One warm afternoon, quite late in the day,
I attended a clinic - yes, one where you pay,
The doctor arrived, a really nice chap,
I told him I'd come with a pain in my back.

The doc asked some questions then took a
look
At my head, legs and feet and right hand that
shook.
He watched while I walked, then came back
again.
He said "I know your problem, you've lost
half your brain."

"You're a Parky" he said "Now that's quite
good news"
"You'll live long and prosper, I'm telling the
truth".
So I thought long and hard to find something
funny
To tell my two lads what's wrong with their
Mummy.

Remembering Christmas, that's first on my
list,
'Cos to beat up the cream my hand was a
whisk,
Then mopping the wine which I'd spilt on
the floor
Like the water I spilled and the tea - there'll
be more!

But so far the best thing of all for us Parkys
Is joining with others at The Parkinson Soci-
ety,
Meeting new friends who don't mind if we
dribble,
Or are slow when we're walking, or write tiny
scribble.

There's Flora and Chris and Maureen and
Tony,
Paul, Alan and Jackie, there's no need to be
lonely.
Just join in the fun. Oh, and Patricks we've
two!
And there's Betty and Pat. I'm so glad I
joined you.

We all have "The Problem" but still we can
smile,
Yes, us here in Sevenoaks do it in style.
Seriously though, you're all a good bunch
Now let's settle down and get on with our
lunch!

The Building Project

Sitting in the garden one hot afternoon
A suggestion was made that we needed more room.
I glanced round at Frank, he had a faraway look
So I hurriedly buried my head in my book.

"A conservatory may be nice my dear"
"What, all those windows to clean. No way, no fear!"
"Or maybe an extension, that would be great"
"Not on your life, all that mess, hard luck mate"

Well as time went by a few people heard
The sound of a drill, a cement mixer purred.
Up came the patio, down went the base.
Next came the walls then windows in place,
Doors followed on then the roof was put up,
This while consuming hot tea by the cup...
Every day something different was done
But when he drilled out the wall I did not call it fun!

With plaster and paint and new lights in as well,
A carpet was chosen, yes that would look swell.
At last it was finished – all shiny and new,
He can sit at the table and look at the view.
He's got his extension, my man he's done good!
Now let's cut the tape while the champagnes' still cool.

Forty Years of Fun

It was ten days before Christmas we had our first baby boy,
He came with the presents and brought bundles of joy.
He would sit on his potty one leg in the air,
And sleep on the floor his head under a chair.

We watched, as he grew first learning to talk,
Then falling and bruising while learning to walk.
It was painful to watch but he was tough even then,
He just dried up the tears then fell over again.

His brother arrived when he was two and a half
And eighteen months later they played a guitar.
The photo looks good but the sound was too flat,
They would **NOT** be pop stars, no doubt about that.

When school came along he took that in his
stride,
Wore his uniform daily and wore it with
pride.
Told his teacher "One day I'll be a doctor,
you'll see"
He replied, "With your brains you won't –
but you might make their tea".

He brought home an ashtray found in the
woods
It was rusty and dirty and not very good.
But with spit and polish and rubbing like
mad,
It shone as he smiled and said Happy Birth-
day Dad.

Here he's digging the garden, there's a fork in
his hand,
A good job we don't have to live off the land!
With his friends he went fishing, now stories
get bigger,
He smelt to high heaven and fell asleep in his
dinner.

He swam for his club and the county and
school,
Winning medals – By the way there's a brick
in the wall
With his name on, it says for charity he'd run.
His name's upside down, reading that should
be fun.

As the years were passing there was college
then work.
It was then we decided our son was a berk.
He let his hair grow, how long would it get?
So long that in bed he wore a hair net.

At twenty the craze became motorbikes,
I preferred days when he just rode a trike.
His friends who were bikers were not really
bad,
Just rock loving, beer drinkers – yes, totally
mad.

He went to the bank, a loan to arrange
For a new Kawasaki, top of the range.
With holes in his pockets and holes in his
shoes,
All stuck with **duck tape** - how could they
refuse.

One night in a pub a girl caught his eye,
He asked for a date, thought he'd give her a
try.
First she played hard to get, but then she
gave in.
And before very long she had also moved in.

His stag night arrived; it was off to the sea
Where they covered him in treacle, from his
head to his knees.
Stuck grass, sand and pebbles all over his bod
Hoping he'd be arrested by a bright P C Plod.

Then he married Maria, a wife he adores,
And we struck quite lucky; she's our daughter in law.
She kept him quite busy, changed the boy to a man.
He took up ju-jitsu and is now a black Dan.

They found time for babies, two girls then two boys,
At Christmas they're broke as they go hunting for toys.
So fast do they grow, they need new shoes and coats,
And their antics are legend, too many to note.

We look now to Trevor our new entrepreneur
As he works really hard to make their future secure.
It is fun now to watch, see those wrinkles appear.
But we are proud to request you – Please - give Trevor a cheer!

    (What a party that was!!)

A Very Special Day

So Gary has finally done it
He's decided to name the day
He's agreed that he will get married
And with Helen he will spend his days.

And Helen, well she's also done it
She's finally caught her man
And the punishment she must endure
Is to be part of the Henderson Clan.

We hope they will be very happy
We know that in days to come
They will both look at one another
And say, God, WHAT have we done?

Come the patter of tiny feet
The bathing and changing of nappies
And lack of a good nights sleep
We hope they'll still feel very happy

But with love and deep understanding
They will steadily make their way
Along the path we've all trodden before them
We wish them Good Luck on their Wedding day

My Jackdaws

Sometimes I would laugh and sometimes I have been quite exasperated with Franks' unending hoard of junk. I say junk intentionally but to Frank it is invaluable. He often comes home with a box full of bits and pieces: all sorts of metal, screws and wire, a cupboard with no paint on it, probably found in someone's garden, would look lovely here or there.

Of course when I have seen it usually, it goes there, there being the shed!

I must admit sometimes something will come in useful, there have been occasions when some small piece will be just what we need to repair the coffee table, or invariably when a doorknob is needed Frank will find one in his "invaluables".

I used to wonder when the boys were small, just how they would grow up. People always say they take after their Mum or Dad and

everyone says Trevor takes after me. This I
have contradicted time and again but now, lo
and behold, at the tender age of seven Trevor
has discovered Frank's infatuation for collect-
ing.
Today I suppose you would say, he has begun
his apprenticeship.

He arrived home from school wreathed in
smiles but with a touch of mystery about
him.
Clutching a rather bulky object in his coat he
announced proudly, he had a present for
Daddy, definitely just what he wants. And
with a flourish there was a rather rusty, solid
old ashtray, found on the way home from
school.

Where, on the journey home could only have
been down the FORBIDDEN woods, and
judging from the dirty shoes, I knew my
assumption was correct, though before I
could deal with that I had to finish the ash-
tray problem.

Having pointed out it was second hand and
really, I thought we might do a bit better than
that. I felt some degree of surprise to see the
same obstinate look as Frank gives me, come
flashing in my direction accompanied by the
announcement that, with some cleaning and

polishing afterwards it will be fine for the car passenger seat. The fact that it cost nothing just adds to the attraction.

It is now hidden away until he can accomplish the transformation without Dad emerging on the scene.

There is just one thing nagging at the back of my mind at the moment.
If Trevor is following in Frank's footsteps just where will we put all his junk, sorry, useful articles. Frank has already filled most available space? MOVE?

A Tale of a Roaming Rascal

This is a tale of a young man about twenty,
Of pretty young girls for him there were plenty,
But for choice he was spoiled, which one should he choose?
He was tired of wondering and went off for a snooze.
He dreamed of far places, saw such beauty to behold.
On waking he knew he'd go digging for gold.
While travelling he will try Thailand's exotic food
And if he makes it to OZ he'll have a taste for their booze.

So our friend Bruce's going on a trip to Thai
With the next stop Australia, if the plane will still fly.
B.A., Caledonian, Qantas, they'll all fight
To eject drunken Bruce with all of their might.
But with him as a passenger the crew could run amok

The hostesses all fighting to show him Bang-
kok.

With a girl on each arm and a drink in each
hand
They will show him around this colourful
land.
He'll meet girls who wear skirts slit to the
waist
And make it their pleasure to learn Bruce's
tastes.
They will pamper and spoil him, give him
massages free,
In fact these are extras supplied with the tea.

The day will arrive, he'll have had quite
enough
Of this life of seduction and 'nookie' and
stuff.
So he'll send for his bill saying he will depart,
Then find that on sex he's spent all his Thai
baht.
So to jail he will go and this time he will see
How wise to have cards to 'get out of jail
free'.

So it's off now to OZ to find old Dundee
To see if he's hiding behind a gum tree.
To hunt through the bush and meet Abbo's
who'll say
"Hello there, it's Bruce, how are you, g' day."

He'll look for the crocs and show them his
knife.
They'll be scared out their skins and run for
their life.
Then he'll find old Dundee and show him
some skins
But all he'll be wanting is tins, tins and tins
Of Fosters, the lager that reaches the brain
And Bruce will be back on the drink once
again.
Back to the booze, to his usual state
And maybe a fight with his drunken old
mate.

Back to a cell for a sobering up
And realisation he has run out of luck.
Dreaming of Chelsea loosing at home
He decides he must settle and no more will
he roam.
So he'll find him a Sheila, so blonde and so
fair,
He'll raise six drunken kids and settle down
there.

When nearing Ninety and burned by the sun
That crafty red spider will bite Bruce's bum.
And he'll be remembered long after he's gone
As loveable Bruce, that old drunken POM!!!

Carnival Time down Tonbridge Way

It was the second time the Tonbridge crowd
Drove through the high street, shouting loud.
"Look out Tonbridge we are going to win".
"We'll put the rest of you in a flat spin".

It is Carnival time and we've spent a few
hours
Thinking of rhymes, and we've made lots of
flowers.
A slogan was chosen "A legend in Insurance"
But after our efforts seemed more "A legend
in Endurance."

We had the Mad Hatters Tea Party, where tea
turned to wine.
Where Mr Prebble plus hat, had a whale of a
time.
Alice was asking the way though the door,
But she was so pickled she stayed on the
floor.

18

There were Kelvin and Joy our King and our Queen,
The King on his throne was a sight to be seen.
His throne was a loo and with shouts of "Oh No"
He'd sit down and say "I've just got to GO".

With so many people, our Cards and our Hare,
The Drink Me, and Eat Me, our Knave, he was rare.
Rabbit's watch stuck at Ten to Two,
The Queen chopping heads – that's all she could do!

With all this happening we were sure we would win,
But after the judging we all lost our grin.
After all our efforts we had not won
But we all agreed it was such tremendous FUN.

An Arresting Occasion

When Tony awakened one September morn
He thought he would celebrate the day he
was born,
In his tried and tested and time honoured
way
With some alcohol beverage around mid-day.
The morning dragged on but at twelve on the
dot
He put down his pen, made his usual inkblot.
On with his jacket and off to the pub,
Plenty to drink and a large plate of grub.

He staggered back at a quarter to three
Then promptly was sent for everyone's tea.
Back at his desk pandemonium broke out
As blowing her whistle and giving a shout
A policewoman cried "Is Tony Marshall here?
I just want to take your particulars dear".

"Your cars badly parked and I'm P C Whip"
And without more ado she started to strip.
She took off her tunic, her shirt and her tie.
At this point in time Tony wanted to die.

She put his hands upon his head
Then showed him her garter "It's yours" she said,
"But you must remove it without using your hands".
We could sense the adrenalin reaching his glands.

He nibbled away with obvious glee
And succeeded in taking this prize from her knee.
She posed for some pictures to record the fun
The lads joining in. But what had Paul done?
She called him over using his name
And we really know just what IS her game.

The photographs taken, her clothes all put on
With a hug and a kiss our lady was gone.
Now our decrepit old colleague is now
twenty eight.
Well done Tony, You really were GREAT!!

Hitching a Lift Down Under

My name is Kanga but they call me Roo
And there is something I would like you to
do.
When you go on your travels with the bags
you have packed,
Please take my baby to the Great Outback.
In the land where the sun shines most of the
day,
Show him the place where Koala bears play.
Where the Wallaby go 'walk about', and
Abo's go too,
Where they hunt for their food, and then play
Didgeridoo.
Look at the Coral Reef, see how it glows,
Then on to the shore where the Mango tree
grows.
When you have seen all the sites it will be
about May.
Time for the train ride then, call it a day.
Back to the airport: your flights booked for
June,
Yes, Waltzing Matilda's a memorable tune.

You may hum it and sing it we will not com-
plain,
Just don't choose a journey this far again.
By now 'little Roo' won't fit in my pouch
And if he tries to get back I swear I'll scream
– Ouch!!!

The Return

Six months are up and your home again
Gosh how we prayed you would catch that
plane.
The letters came back, the news travels fast
While we were left wondering if your money
would last.
You have now been to places we'll never see
Like the Barrier Reef and the Mango tree.
You have snorkelled and dived
Did you have a 'Roo ride?
You have slept with the bugs
And had Aussies hugs.
You sold a picture and advertisement space,
Then went to Cairn with a packed suitcase.
Alice Springs had a visit
Then you started to fidget
To see more of these places
With wide open spaces.
During these travels it was birthday time
And we couldn't even drop you a line
Now this trip has ended you'll have memories
galore.
And if you think you'll go again we will bolt
the door.

She is Off Again!

So Julie your off on your travels, this time a
trip to Hong Kong,
I knew you would have to go wandering but
do you have to go for so long?
I just hope the postman remembers where we
live, so he'll find the right door
For your letters, or maybe a card to land on
the mat on the floor.
When you took off before for Australia, I
knew we would meet up again
But if Hong Kong's a place to delight you,
you might miss the England bound plane.
I hope you'll be happy and have fun in Bang-
kok or even Taiwan.
Just remember, you wanted six kids in your
life, so come back or end up as a nun.

Saturday Surprise

The alarm radio burst into life with the sound of Winter Wonderland being played. Putting my head under the covers I pretended not to hear, but this ploy didn't work and I was rudely poked and told it was my turn to make the tea. Then I remembered, it was Saturday and I had agreed to work, so I opened one eye and realised the room was extra bright. It had snowed. Not just a light fall but quite deep.

I jumped out of bed, envious of my husband tucking himself down in the warm. Perhaps the road will be impassable, perhaps the ice will be too bad, perhaps I can stay at home too, perhaps.........

After taking the tea up to the family and finishing my usual ablutions, I ventured outside. The council had already done a grand job clearing the snow and although the roads were icy they were clear enough to try to get through.

I set off for work, but not before I had given the family a list of jobs to be done, with a special plea for the hall decorating to be finished!

Travelling was hazardous but I arrived in one piece and started the day's tasks. All went well and I was finished by half past three. Phoning home before I left to tell them I was on my way and should be home by half past four, I thought my message was not greeted with much enthusiasm. Probably they would just be starting their jobs and would be trying desperately to finish before I arrived. Oh well, at least the dinner will be ready for me. I drove towards our house intending to park carefully, when my attention was caught by something in the garden.

I was so shocked I nearly ran over it! There was a snowman sitting fishing, holding a rod, with a big notice wishing all fisher folk a "Happy Christmas and New Year." Opening the front door I was greeted by a sheepish husband and two sons. "Sorry about the jobs Mum, but we've been busy outside."

"I can see that, he almost fills the front garden"

"No, that one is Dad's it took him ALL DAY!!" "Come with us!"

There in the back garden were the results of their efforts. The snowman's wife.

Grandpa's 60th Birthday

(Performed by granddaughters Sabrina 6 and Jordan 4)

Our Grandpa's having a birthday
He is getting on a bit
But even though he is sixty
He is keeping very fit.

He can throw Dad over his shoulder
And catch Mum when she runs
But we know he is getting older
'Cos he says we weigh half a ton.

So let's enjoy the party
A barbeque has begun
Happy Birthday Grandpa
Let's keep having lots of fun!

We have had BBQs in our garden for many occasions. I promised Marion a BBQ if she recovered from an operation. The Park referred to is Frimley Park Hospital.

Welcome Home Marion!

We all know that Marion's been poorly,
She went to Cyprus and got sick,
She came back in a hurry
With a pain in her tummy
And her back and a few other bits.

Back home in Frimley the Park kept her in.
The Doc looked her over, said "Gosh, where've you been?"
He prodded and poked
Showed his colleagues her notes
And a scan showed an alien "thing".

They opened her up and what a surprise,
Out bounced a ball in front of their eyes,
She'd swallowed it whole while shouting hooray!!

She'd gone up to Wembley to watch Carling
play.
Now what will she do to fulfil her dreams?
How about training, with this gorgeous team.

*The team were male members of the family –
all ages, dressed in a mix match of kit.
None looked like Will Carling! But they
made her feel good!*

Lisa Comes of Age

In 1967 down East Peckham way
There was joyous shouting "Hip Hip Hoo-
ray"
To the Papworths was born a baby girl
And to Mum and Dad she was a beautiful
pearl!

She was very good and by the time she was
two
She was three foot high and her feet grew
and grew.
But those twinkling toes weren't allowed to
slack
They were quickly taught how to dance and
to tap.

While learning at school 'tho not very wise
Her writing was awarded a "commendable"
prize.
A skill soon forgotten I hasten to add
You try to decipher the notes on her pad!!

Then to college for cooking but this didn't
last
She wanted some wages and left very fast.
Into insurance at Lombard she came
And life in accounting was never the same.

When she goes for the coffees she dances a
jig
Now she's moved to statistics, that task is
quite big.
There's the fund for the Pandas, so now we
can't swear
And some of us find that just too much to
bear.

But her skills are in cakes and what beauties
there's been
With a Bungalow, Sports bag and Big Mac to
be seen.
Now she goes to the pub, her life's on the
skid
The new name she is known by is "The
Brandy Kid."

Now she's reached twenty one she is coming
of age
What gift can we give her on our meagre
wage?
There's just one gift for her - Her dream
come true.
"Lisa, Happy Birthday - Here's Joseph for
you!"

*Lisa has seen the show Joseph a lot so enter a
colleague in flowing colourful coat secretly
made in the office*

"You've been to the show five times or more
And you are the one who shouts ENCORE
You came to Guildford and gave me a rose
Its perfume still lingers just under my nose.
But one thing is wrong - no I'm not a phoney
My name isn't Joseph just call me TONY."

He ends by giving her a rose

Some Come and Some Go

It was somewhere about nineteen eighty two,
Lombard wasn't sure just what to do.
We had new management coming in
And when they arrived they caused quite a
din.

Then about October a new boy appeared
He had youthful looks underneath his beard.
Another John, Oh No! We groaned
Three is too many - could they be clones?

But like the others he surely was not,
He was quiet and studious, we liked him a lot.
The work he was given was soon put away
"I will do it tomorrow" he was heard to say.

"One of us" we all agreed
And we took him to Tonbridge with maxi-
mum speed.
He became a dab hand at juggling accounts
Like Trade stats, Marine stats and cheques
that bounce.

When the auditors came he did not go sick
He stayed at his desk, with his work he would stick.
But when the sun shone he was off at the double
To meet Cathy his wife, if stopped there was trouble.

Off to the golf course both would go.
Did they hole in one? Of course not, oh no!
They would play a few holes and then hurry back
To Rupert John's hound, 'though we think he's a cat.

Back at the office things have started to change
With staff moving on, it's all very strange.
Now Johns not a person you could ever call lazy
But work seemed to turn him a little bit crazy...

A challenge was needed to give him a lift
And Yasuda's come up with a virtual gift.
He is climbing the ladder, he is sure to do well
And will Lombard miss him? Of course! You can tell!

For Karen, — This is James's Life

It was December '69 with Christmas looming
near
That Barbara and Pete's second son decided
to appear.
They already had a lively lad, Timothy is his
name,
What shall we call this lovely boy? Jimbo?
Jim? Nah James!
He brought his parents lots of joy
And Tim thought him the perfect toy.

The years flew by, he was soon at school
The perfect place to act the fool.
But fool he was not and he worked extra hard
To prove he could master the I.T. card.
He found good employment, then time for
fun
He liked BIG Buxom women - or so said his
Mum!

He went up to town dressed up in drag,
With make up and beard, red boots and a
bag!

To the next Rocky Horror he wore red high heeled shoes
And got touched up - what a bargain! He just couldn't loose!
Thank goodness for Karen, let's hope she can cope
With this cross-dressing rocker - a comedian of note.

He shares all he has with Karen, that's a fact
Except for his baby, that's right, Jess the cat.
His romantic approach when he went down on one knee
To propose to Karen, down deep in the sea,
Shows a man who is fun and happy with life,
We know they'll be happy now Karen's his wife.

The Summer Of '54

Life had become rather distressing in my teen years. I had frequently been told they were the best years of your life, but mine had been uneventful, until ………

One evening my brother and his wife said they would take me with them on holiday, to Broadstairs in Kent. With two children this was to be a beach holiday with perhaps a day trip, so I expected a quiet time.

Taking the train from Croydon was fun with the children, their excitement was catching and on arrival at the guest house I felt cheered by the landlady's greeting "Welcome, make yourselves at home. If you need anything just ask. Oh, and by the way baby sitting is part of the service". Good, maybe a trip to the theatre would be possible.

Playing with the children filled our days but the evenings were harder to fill. Our landlady recommended the local dance hall, reminding us of her offer to baby sit. As this was cheaper than the theatre we readily agreed.

Tuesday evening we set off, Dick and Sylvia eager, me apprehensive, sure I would be a sad wallflower.

How was I to know it was the beginning of a taste of freedom and fun?

During the evening I met two lads who kept me on the dance floor most of the night. They were also on holiday and came from Essex, touring in an open top sports car. We arranged to meet the next day. The boys had intended to move on that day but stayed to take me on a tour of the local sights. We went all along the coast to Dover, stopping for lunch, getting me back in time for dinner with my family. Meeting up again later for an evening stroll, (this with NO TIME LIMIT from restrictive parents!)
I can't remember what we laughed at but we seemed to find plenty of things funny so we were sorry the evening had to end.

We said our farewells: they were leaving in the morning.

Next day as we finished breakfast, the land-lady called Dick to one side. "Can Eileen have visitors?" she asked. My friends were back!

Another fun day followed but this time their car broke down miles from anywhere. I never knew you could find pushing a car fun but it was. We finally found a garage that got us going again but it was late before we arrived back at my lodgings. There we found a very concerned brother. We said farewell again and promised to write.

The following day was our last so we prepared for the beach one last time. As we left the building a car drew up, sounding the horn. The boys were grinning from ear to ear saying they wanted us to end the holiday together. Dick and Sylvia looked at me, and seeing my pleading look gave in. I jumped into the car and we were off, me sitting high up on the back of the boot – I forgot to say it was only a two seater. The hours flew by and soon it was all over!

Another wonderful day. Another very late night. Sorry Dick.

This time a farewell, which had to be the last. With an emotional hug to the lads, I waved them off with a tear and a smile.

Thanks Les and Jim for showing me youth can be fun!!

On the train home my brother looked across at me and said,"What are you smiling at?"

"Wouldn't you like to know" was the reply!!

When Richard achieved his Half Century

When Richard Wilkins woke up at dawn
He went back to sleep yes, that was the norm
But very soon Jan gave him a nudge
"Come on get up, your late again love"

He made some tea and fed the cat
Listened for the postman, nothing fell on the mat
After a shower he got in his car
And drove to work, fifteen miles is quite far.

He was feeling his age, his knees started creaking
As he walked up the stairs he heard The Irishman speaking.
"Now, all together, he'll have forgotten the date
Let's give him something to celebrate."

There was the desk decorated with flowers,
A banner, balloons, it took us two hours
It was worth it to see Richard change to a nifty,
Happy smiling young man of fifty!

It was James "The Irishman's" turn next.

Congratulations James on reaching fifty
And just like Richard you're really quite nifty
We know John thinks that though you are
slim
You'd be much better off if you went for a
swim.
He would buy you a ticket, even ferry you
there.
Having done twenty lengths you'll be too
shattered to care.
But you like to garden, out at the crack of
dawn,
"Do you have a meeting with some Lepre-
chaun?"
Having broken your back on the patch that
you dug
Please welcome our nurse - to give you a rub!

Enter a very sexy nurse with a strange potion

With this Ring

Today's the day at last it has arrived
No matter where John runs there's no place
to hide.
Lisa will find him of that we are sure
And from three thirty onwards she will have
bolted the door.

She will have promised to love him 'till death
do them part
And we know that he treasures her with all
his heart.
Then there's photos and cake while friends
say "well done"
After which they will fly to find sand, sea and
sun.

When work days are over and home John is
strolling
A note will be left saying - Sorry, gone bowl-
ing!
But we know they'll survive and be very
happy
When Lisa is up to her elbow in nappies.

So be happy today and have no fear
John and Lisa Bride and Groom of the Year!

Another Couple Tie the Knot

To Susie and Bill we are glad to say
We all hope you have a wonderful day.
We passed round the hat and what a surprise,
Enough for a present to delight your eyes.

Down the market the stalls only had tat,
But the Oxfam shop had some super mats.
There was a goat's rug to put beside your
bed,
But the smell would make Bill think you were
dead!

So we hope this gift is on the right lines,
You can take it to Uncles if you fall on hard
times.
Like you Susie it is quite a nice dish,
To be filled with your fruit or some veg if
you wish.

We hope you'll be happy and your dreams
come true,
As we send our good wishes for the future to
you.

Memories for Joy

Ten years ago Joy you walked through the
door,
Just what to expect I wasn't quite sure.
Kelvin's wife would have charm, style and
flair,
And of course a head of magnificent hair.

But we were not prepared for the smile on
your face
Which Lombard soon changed to a chagrined
grimace.
"You need staff," you were told "just one or
two"
"That will give you something to prove".
"First there is Lisa the new girl, she'll do,
And then there's the "old un" still here for a
year or few."

Well! If only the Governors had known what
they'd done.
We all got together and had so much fun.
The work was the target to be achieved
But it was friendship, which prospered and
was conceived.

The things we have done we'll remember
forever,
Like the Carnival floats. Forget them? No
never!
There was Kelvin in bed in a bowler, and
briefcase.
While you showed your garter to guys who
gave chase,
Their faces consumed with lascivious grins
Which soon disappeared when we rattled our
tins.

The pennies collected gave others some
cheer,
While you agreed to be a queen next year.
We would walk to the George, a regular trip
Where we'd wait for the filling in your sand-
wich to drip.
A messy beef toastie, you could not refuse
But the calorie count – well that was bad
news.

The rehearsal for Christmas when with Lisa
you sang
Dressed as two sexy Santa's. That went with a
BANG.
There was New York, New York, sung with
Annie for John.
Where the wine bar staff watched all that
went on.

And the laughs as we made Tony's coat of
colours,
When as Joseph for Lisa, he did the honours.

There were sad times as well which we took
in our stride.
You showed the way, with compassion and
pride.
And when you read this Joy – Well the "old
un's" still here,
With the memories and your friendship,
which she holds very dear.

Waving Goodbye to Fiona

We all know a girl called Fiona
Who is known as a bit of a loner,
She joined us at Purley
Where we realised quite early
Her nickname was "Prima Mac doughnut"

Now she previously trained as a teacher
Where her knowledge would be used for the
best,
But a total disaster
The kids burst into laughter
When Fiona arrived at her desk.

So she joined us at Lombard quite quickly
Made her mark on the VAT man some say.
But they decided to test her
She got seconded to Spicer and Pegler
Where she stayed for six months and a day.

She moved to a flat at Tunbridge
To St Johns where the toffs congregate.
That left her quite skint
We were all tickled pink
When she shared Lynda's blouse for a date.

She has travelled to far away places
In the States she was her sister's lodger
The Moroccan men
Were like pigs - and should be penned.
She preferred five days in Paris with Roger.

Will she marry this man who has changed
her?
If you look in her eyes you see stars
But if he's a big spender
There is one thing might tempt her
If he replaced her lost company car!

Now Fiona doesn't suffer fools gladly
So she's off to give Cornhill a try.
I don't think I'd be wrong
If we echoed this song.
"We wish you luck as we wave you goodbye!"

The Wrinklies Lament

So our Linda's reached her landmark
She is into her Fortieth year
She is really not wearing too badly
Although signs are beginning to appear.

If you look close at her knee cap
There's a hole where repairs have been done
And though pain was a bit of a set back
The Doctor came second to none!!!

When he looked at her knees he sent tingles
Up her spine, we are led to believe
And it's strange how his powers of healing
Have done wonders for healing those knees.

We must keep ever watchful in future
From her knees the next move is her waist
Then the parts she will next need repairing
Will end up at the top - yes, her face.
When her wrinkles are short lived and vanish
And her grey hairs turn brown overnight
We all know that the years after forty
Can be fun, simply filled with delight!!

A Christmas Tale

It was December and very cold when the young boy walked out of the Job centre. Once again there was nothing on offer. He turned towards the park, walking briskly to keep warm, but as he hadn't eaten he soon felt cold and tired. He sat on a bench to rest and soon a pretty girl about sixteen years old joined him. She was pretty, but there was something wrong, he thought she would look lovely if only her eyes would sparkle.

After settling herself she opened her bag and took out some papers. They were about the YTS Scheme. "That's interesting" the lad said, "You should try that".

"Nobody would want to take me on" she replied "I haven't done very well at school and Mum said "No work, no room!" They decided to keep each other company. Looking for somewhere to stay they started to walk out of the park.

Turning the corner they bumped into a man in a hurry. "Why don't you look where your going?" the boy said angrily. He was taut and the girl noticed his fist. "Don't clench your fists, he'll think you are threatening him" she whispered.

"Clench, Clench, how do you know my name is Clench?" said the man.

"We don't Sir. We are just looking for some shelter, can you help?" they replied.

"I'm afraid not, but I will give you some advice; be kind to animals and you will be alright." and the man hurried away.

Feeling hungry they looked for some nuts to eat, the squirrels had only left a few but the boy threw some to a baby squirrel and watched him dash away.

When they reached the main road they heard a loud bang, turning just in time to see a car ram another and roar off. At this point a man came running towards them. "The owner will have a shock when he sees his car has been pranged" said the boy.

"Laing, Laing, how do you know my name is Laing?" he asked.

"We don't Sir, but I can tell you the number of the other car. We are just looking for food and shelter."

"Well thank you. All I can offer you is a stale sandwich and my advice; be kind to animals and you will be looked after."

The man had come from a building and round the back there was some wasteland, the young couple decided to rest for the night under the trees. They shared the sandwich and gave the crust to some birds. The girl had just got settled when a bird left his calling card. "Oh ****" she said.

"I know it is but there's no need to swear".

Their raised voices attracted the attention of a man who had parked his car in the adjacent car park. "I am sorry" she said "We were having a tiff".

"Smith, Smith, how do you know my name is Smith?" he asked.

"We don't Sir, we are looking for work and shelter." they replied. He gave them a blanket from his car saying "That's all I have and my advice; don't be hard on animals, look after them and you will be taken care of. Goodnight." and away he went.

In the morning they were woken by a car being parked. A man walked into the building. A few minutes later another man ran to the car and tried the door. He was trying to break the lock with a piece of wire. Creeping stealthily the young couple caught him and while the girl raised the alarm the boy pinned the thief to the ground.

After the thief had been dealt with, the owner of the car asked to speak to the young couple.

"What were you doing on our property?" he asked.

"Sheltering for the night. We are now going to look for work, then we can both go back home."

"Well that can be arranged" the man said handing them a card "I am the General Manager of this company. You will both be offered a position here. Welcome to Care 4 Animals, suppliers of all pet foods and owners of small holdings for beginners. You are just the people we need."

Out on the pavement, wreathed in smiles the girl said "Now I understand why the three wise men said be kind to animals, that mans name is Mr Lamb".

"We will have a Happy Christmas!!"

The Garden

As I wander round our garden
It shows signs of clear neglect,
The weeds have all grown rampant
While the thistles stand erect.

The bindweed has taken over,
Our shrubs, they're covered in blight,
Then I turn to a bed full of roses
Now they are a glorious sight.

Without our care and protection
They have grown almost seven feet tall,
Every stem being heavy and blooming
Making carpets of colour where petals fall.

Our holiday trips have been costly,
Now the garden needs putting to right.
We hurriedly weed, trim and water,
With the bindweed we have quite a fight.

Our work is soon showing improvement
By removal of weeds and dead stuff.
Very soon we can sit and admire
Our garden and say, "Whew, that's enough!"

The Big Birthday

As I sit here dreaming I wonder, how will tomorrow be?
I am having another birthday and I won't be twenty three.
Now, that year was a good one, I was a newly married wife
Who was going to have a baby, to change the rest of my life.

These were happy years (washing nappies) as we watched our family grow,
By twenty six we had two boys, now I was kept on the go.
At thirty one I had a third son, though this was not meant to be
I knew I would never have the feeling of him climbing upon my knee.

The following years of my thirties were probably some of the best,
I had learnt from life's early lesson to be happy with our boys in our nest.
My forties passed quietly, though busy with a husband and two teenage lads.

When the days' work was done, we had
plenty of fun; to some we seemed quite mad.

In my fifties my sons became fathers, making
families of their own.
How I missed them playing their music and
bringing weird friends to our home.
So we moved to a place in the country, where
work began again,
My fifties soon became sixties when I won-
dered, was I insane?

I had been working and feeling quite poorly,
it was time to take a rest,
So retirement came with a plan, it was time it
was put to the test.
Go on tour with our caravan and travel to
places far and wide,
At sixty six to France we went, for a trip of
nine weeks there to hide.

It was great and I soon felt quite better and
to do it again was a must.
At sixty eight our ferry was booked, this time
for twelve weeks or bust.
I was there for my sixty ninth birthday, what
trophy could I obtain?
Climb a mountain? Yes we did it! But next
time we go on the train!

Well the big one has come and gone now,
"how would it be" I had asked,
No, I didn't want a party and these years have flown by quite fast.
A quiet meal for two would be nice, down south, in France, by the Med.
So many miles – could we make it? The reply was a shake of the head.

We set off for France with a map and a schedule we needed to keep,
There were some delays on our journey that slowed us for more than a week,
But we arrived just in time for our dinner, by the Med. At Banyul-sur-Mere
Where we enjoyed my reaching seventy by celebrating with fireworks and flair!

Our family have enjoyed many years camping and caravanning and making friends and *travelling. The following poems were written for our local club but you never know, you might like to try it yourselves.*

Caravanning - The Beginning

One year we headed for Scotland
We had hired a caravan we could tow,
We had always borrowed a tent before
Would we again? Oh no!

Our family consists of the two of us
Plus Trevor and Gary our sons,
And camping with comforts of a caravan
Was sure to be lots of fun.

The boys were soon given their daily tasks,
Emptying the rubbish and fetching the water.
Yes, do it each day without being asked.
How we laughed as we heard "Nothing al-
ters".

We went sightseeing and hunted for Nessie
Who is reported to live in a Loch.
When we called she was out! So we fished for
some trout,
And watched the sun setting low from some
rocks.

We arrived the next day at a river
With a rope bridge for getting across.
This was the life for two lively lads
And I liked it too 'till I slipped on some
moss!

The two weeks were quickly over
The caravan was only on loan.
"Can we do this again Dad? Please can we?"
Begged our boys, as we made our way home.

Caravanning – part 2

It was August we holidayed in Scotland,
Towing a caravan, which we had loaned.
We all agreed there was a desperate need
For our family to purchase their own.

By September the pennies were mounting
But surely not nearly enough,
It was pounds we should have been counting.
So we worked extra hard - It was tough!

In October we saw what we wanted
And purchased our first caravan.
Packed sleeping bags, pillows and teabags.
We were off for the start of our plan.

Ramsgate for our first trip was chosen,
We arrived at the site rather late.
Without blankets and gas we were frozen
So till spring we decided to wait.

The next year it really took off,
By then we had learned a few things.
How tow ball grease gets on your trousers
And extra gas everyone brings.

After these lessons have all been learned,
It was off to the show at Earls court.
We check with the bank to see to how much
we'd earned,
Enough! Now a **NEW** van can be bought.

The salesman really was charming
And the caravan truly superb,
We must wait for collection till spring
Which we hope will be March the third.

Caravanning - part 3

After our visit to "The Show" in October
Our patience was put to the test.
But in March our long wait was over,
Our new van had arrived. (We know – you'd
guessed)

We were eager to try our new toy,
And at Romsey were a group from the club.
Frank met a man there he knew as a boy,
While the East Surrey youth took our lads to
the pub.

We learned a lot more that weekend,
And after Romsey our next trip was Sway,
There was Leeds Castle and Swanage and
Send.
For all callers a note said quite briefly–Their
Away!

We have friends we have met with at Easter
For hot cross buns and the Ladies in Bon-
nets,

Then all through the months 'til December,
When by Christmas we've all empty pockets.

With East Surrey we've helped to raise
money,
For charities, some large and some small.
With a fete held in June we pray for the sun,
And welcome all friends to look at our stalls.

There have been trips all over the country,
To foreign lands we have travelled as well.
So guess where I'm writing this poem?
From France! But that's another tale to tell.

(Wardens at Play – Slinfold Volunteers)

The Caravan Club have some beautiful sites
Where you can take your van for a while,
You telephone to book at a place you may
like
Where you're greeted by wardens with wel-
coming smiles.

Now some sites make plenty of money
But some hardly any at all
And one such is Slinfold, that's not a worry
"The Volunteers" just need a call.

We signed to work for a two week term
Hoping we could keep up the pace.
Our colleagues being younger learn quicker
than us,
But then learning computers – they cannot
be raced.

Speaking of racing – tractors come to mind,
The men being cool and collected.
Us girls couldn't wait, Ann went right round
the bend

Then fast down the straight as her steering
was quickly corrected.

Then Eric was heard shouting with glee
"A motor home's stuck in the mud"
The tractor was needed "Quick where's the key?"
He grinned and the tractor gave it a tug!

A few days later while cutting the grass
Frank found a sorry sight,
A seasonal pitch had somehow been passed
And the caravan left in a terrible plight.

The van needed moving and all soon agreed
To walk with the awning attached
Up came pegs, poles held high, we walked at
a gathering speed,
The T.V. Arial carried by me was a sight you
needed to see!
There's a hundred and one jobs the volun-
teers do
Like making the tea and the coffee,
We empty the bins at four after noon,
So the visitors can snooze and snore softly.

There's the daily battle for the tractor
When we collect bottles and empty the bins,
Flush down the drains at the point for water,
But the Elsan pit - is the best prize to win!
You should see us weeding and cleaning
And meeting caravans with a smile,
And when they all leave or we shut for the
evening,
We look at the birds and rest for a while.

Has it been fun you might ask us,
Well laughter still rings in our ears,
Our problems were sorted without any fuss
So our new friends and us can't wait for next
year!

Slinfold Volunteers 2

We arrived once again our rota to do
At this beautiful site where there's rest for a
few.
It was sunny and warm, the weather we like
And we watched as the campers rode off on
their bikes.

As the days got hotter and the sun still ap-
peared
It even bleached my husband's beard.
The sight of us wardens wilting away
Had people praying for rain – 'tho not the
next day!

The rain came down in the middle of the
night,
To thunder we woke, then a lightening strike.
It seemed so near we expected to see
A hole in the office, or a burnt out tree.

No damage was found and the sun tried to
shine.
Then after a while – about a quarter to nine,
The campers courageously ventured out
The storm then returned – they came back all
washed out.

By day three we got used to the regular greet-
ing
"Ooh it's too hot for me love, you must be
melting"
The visitors left for their pitch in a hurry
To arrange their chairs where they thought it
most sunny.

We booked in enough vans to fill our site
Which made us quite tired as day turned to
night.
The remedy for this was to play a C.D.
For us it was Chopin, Brahms and Satie.

Then Margaret and I had a manual to read,
I held it up so she could proceed.
Just at that moment my tremor kicked in
So reading the book made Margaret's eyes
spin.

After a moment her dizziness passed,
We ably completed a difficult task.
She took my laughter with plenty of grace
But now when my shake starts there's a smile
on her face.

A gentleman arrived with his lady
Said he was Chief Druid from Stonehenge
(maybe?)

We assembled and all touched our forelocks
Then presented him with one of our rocks.

On leaving us early one morning
We said our goodbyes through stifled yawn-
ing.
Still laughing he said he had loved his greet-
ing
And looked forward to our very next meet-
ing.

The next day the men cannot be found
Then from the bin area came a sound.
Looking behind the gate where the sound led
Were two dirty men – Boys behind the bike
shed?

A hidden meter was the reason
As water figures needed to be taken,
The dirty "old boys" needed a scrub
Next month the job goes to two more mugs!

The heat wave has passed, we now have a
breeze,
Which may be the cause of Stewart's big
sneeze.
Our second year's over and all is well
We hope to be back next year, I hope you can
tell!

What shall we do today dear?

I ask as I climb out of bed.
"Well I thought we could take a trip love"
"But don't worry your little old head."

"What are we doing today dear?"
I ask as I butter some bread.
"Well I'm pulling the caravan out love "
"But don't worry your little old head".

"Where are we going today dear?"
I ask, as the map needs to be read.
"Well I'll find us a site by the sea love"
"But don't worry your little old head"

"What shall we do here today dear?"
I ask looking for fruit and veg.
"Well I'll wind the legs and fetch water dear".
"But don't worry your little old head".

"What shall we do here today dear?"
I ask as we are now both well fed.
"Well I'll put our seats in the sun dear"
"So don't worry your little old head".

"What shall we do now today dear?"
I ask as the sun's burnt my head.
"Well we'd better pack up and go home love."
"Don't you worry your little old head."

"What shall we do tomorrow dear?"
I ask as I climb back into bed,
"Don't ask! I'll unpack the caravan love"
"While you snuggle down in your bed!"

Halcyon Days

Now I'm retired and still in my prime
I have the reasons and have the time
To visit friends, some old and some new,
But, is this the thing I am anxious to do?

I rise quite early and make some tea,
Wake up my wife with a kiss and a squeeze.
Look at the weather it looks dry and fine.
Yes, I've the reason and yes, I've the time.

Pack a few things in a bag, like a bun,
A drink, some fruit and a hat for the sun.
Look at my wife who is sleeping again.
Remember my jacket just in case it should
rain.

Placing the things in the car for my trip
I am feeling quite frisky, in my step there's a
skip.
Am I going to visit these friends I should
see?
No, I'm off to go fishing - perhaps catch our
tea.

I arrive at a lake and look all about,
There are ducks, there are swans, but no sign
of trout.
I fish on the bank; it's quite hot in the sun,
Then try in a boat. Gosh this fishing is fun!

I fish in the shallows and then in the deep
And wonder if my wife is still sound asleep.
Look at the time, she'll be up and about
And finding me gone she'll be busy no
doubt.

Oh where are those fish, don't they like my
new fly?
And look at those swallows flying high in the
sky.
The day passes quickly; the hours have flown,
Now is the time to wend my way home.

The evening is late, the time nearly ten.
My wife is now furious, dinners ruined again!
No fish did I catch, none leapt on my rod.
Our visit to friends? Perhaps tomorrow -
Please God!!

"Smile - they did!"

Eileen Henderson
2006